I0606004

This Is Why You SWEAT

Dana Peabody

An imprint of PHOENIX International Publications, Inc.

Artwork © Shutterstock 2025 Pixoode; Thomas M Perkins; Max kegfire; Davidenco; robuart; Ka Han; Zdenek Sasek; Gregory Johnston; Pixel-Shot; Ground Picture; Oleg Mikhaylov; kornnphoto; Danny Smythe; Tatuasha; Adisak Riwkratok; ace03; poltu shyamal; Sudowoodo; sasirin pamai; fizkes; farzand01; VikiVector; Kyuubisa; Prostock-studio; Anatoliy Karlyuk; Ale Fernandes; Happy Together; sruilk; Leestudio; SChompoongam; GSDesign; Markus Mainka; Zakir61; Passakorn Umpornmaha; komkrit Preechachanwate; nuwatphoto; travelview

Published by Sequoia Kids Media,
an imprint of Sequoia Publishing & Media, LLC

Sequoia Publishing & Media, LLC,
a division of Phoenix International Publications, Inc.

8501 West Higgins Road, Chicago, Illinois 60631
34 Seymour Street, London W1H 7JE
Heimhuder Straße 81, 20148 Hamburg

CustomerService@PhoenixInternational.com

www.PhoenixInternational.com

Library of Congress Control Number: 2024952488

ISBN: 979-8-7654-1134-6

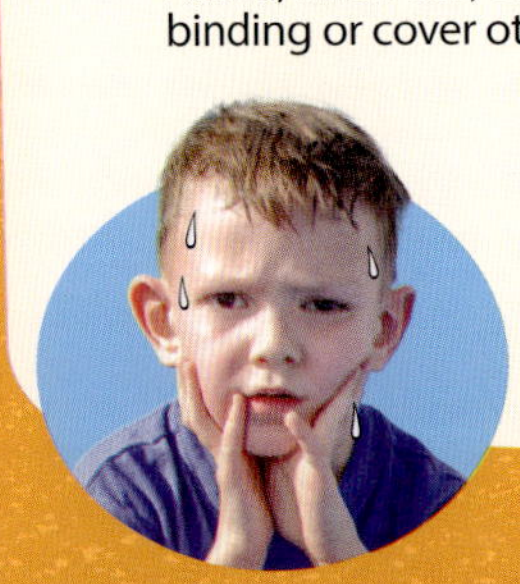

This Is Why You SWEAT

Table of Contents

Bold words are explained in the glossary.

Are you Feeling Warm?

Have you ever gotten a bit warm and noticed your body getting sticky and wet in certain places?

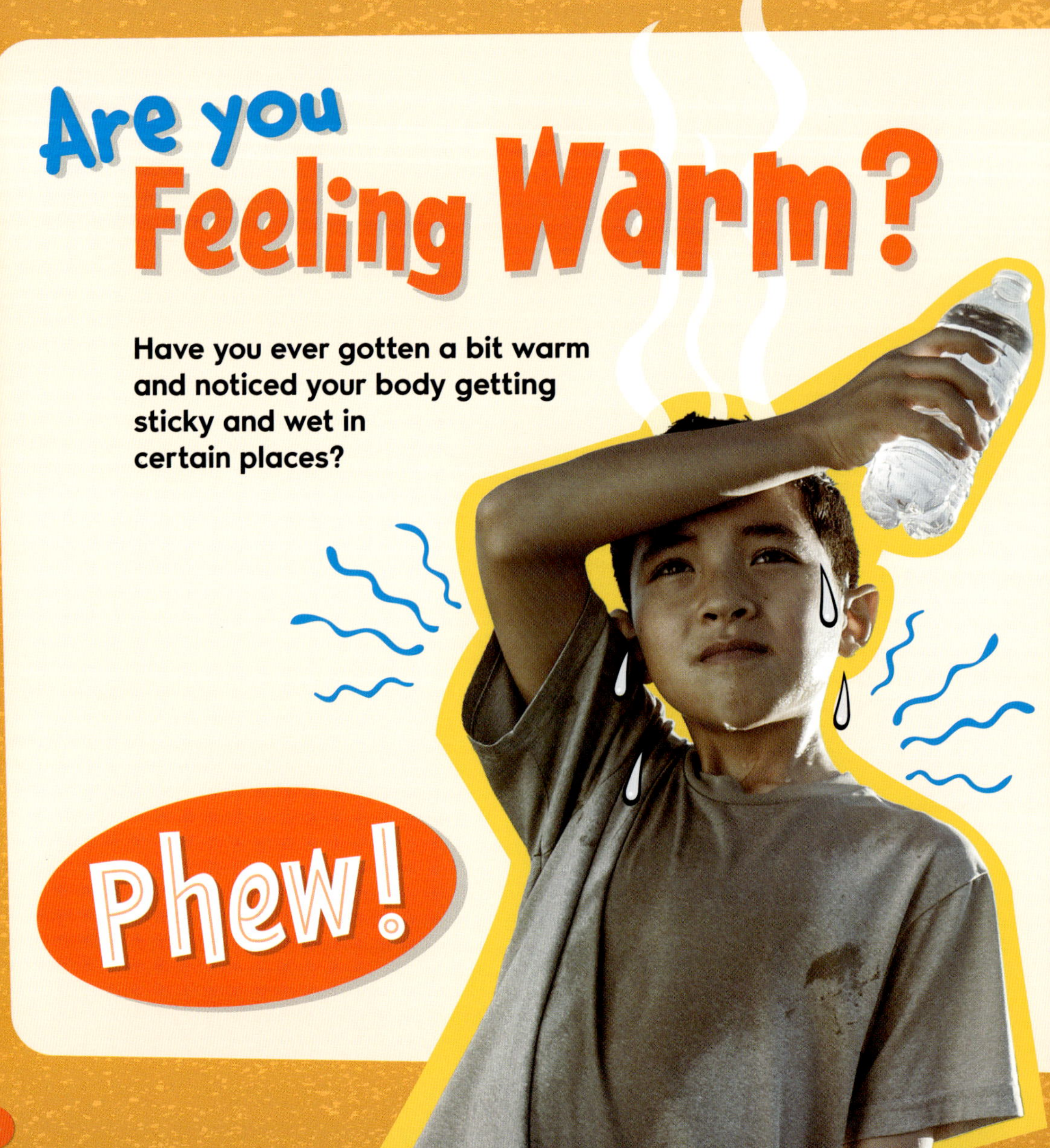

We can sweat for lots of different reasons. Sometimes it is because of the temperature. Sometimes we sweat as a reaction to our emotions.

We need to sweat in order to keep our bodies at the right temperature. If our bodies get too warm, sweating helps us cool down.

Our bodies should be around 98 degrees Fahrenheit (37 degrees Celsius).

As we sweat, our skin becomes wet with **liquid**. This liquid turns into a **vapor** as it leaves our skin. This process is called evaporation (ee-vap-or-ay-shun).

Keep It Level

Sweating is an example of homeostasis (home-ee-oh-stay-sis). Homeostasis is the method our bodies use to keep lots of different things at the right levels.

If the environment changes around us, homeostasis makes sure that it won't affect our bodies on the inside. For example, if we get hot, we sweat to cool down.

If we get cold, we shiver to warm up.

Where Do we Sweat?

Most humans have between two million and five million sweat **glands** all over their bodies. Here are some of the sweatiest places on the body.

There are two main types of glands that make sweat: ECCRINE glands and APOCRINE glands.

Forehead

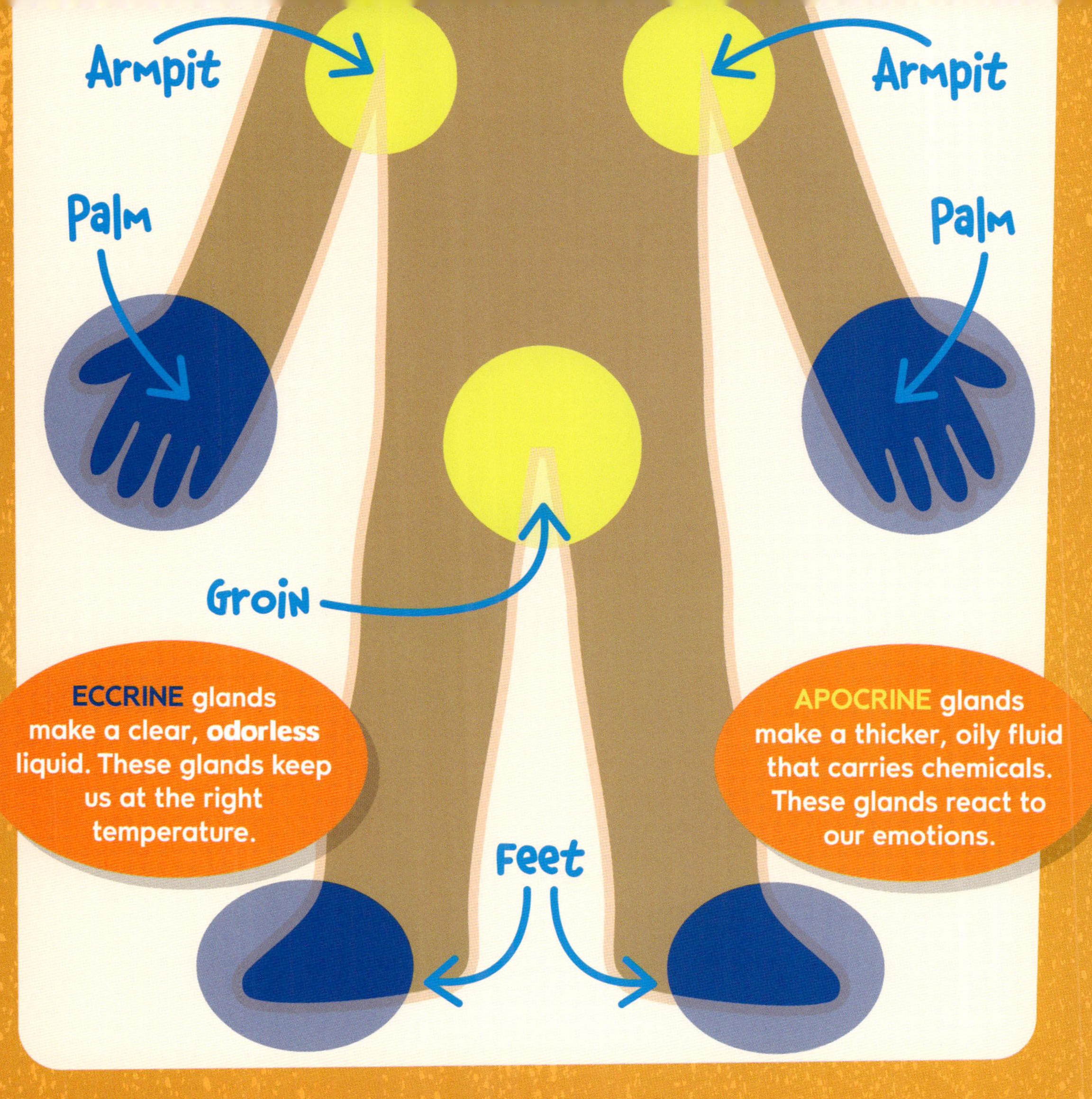
Armpit
Armpit
Palm
Palm
Groin
ECCRINE glands make a clear, **odorless** liquid. These glands keep us at the right temperature.
APOCRINE glands make a thicker, oily fluid that carries chemicals. These glands react to our emotions.
Feet

Exercise

When we exercise, we are more likely to sweat. This is because exercise raises our body temperature. We lose lots of **minerals** when we sweat.

We have to drink lots of water when we exercise because we lose so much through sweating.

Feeling Feverish?

Sometimes when we get sick, we might get a high temperature. This might make us sweat. These illnesses could be:

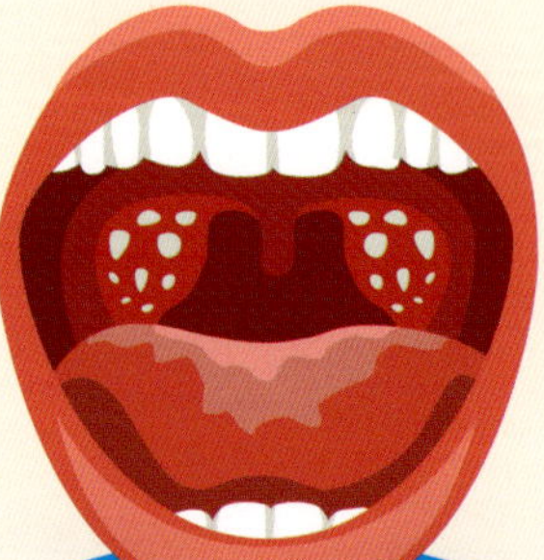

Tonsillitis

Having a high temperature helps fight off nasty illnesses.

Having a high temperature and sweating is one way our body protects us. Lots of **bacteria** and **viruses** that cause illnesses can't survive in very warm bodies.

Cold Sweats

Cold sweats are different from normal sweating. Instead of sweating because your body is too hot, cold sweats are a reaction to other things.

You can get cold sweats for lots of reasons, such as infections, being shocked, or having a sudden fright. These can make your hands and feet clammy.

Fuzzy Bodies

Did you know that you have tiny hairs that cover most of your body? These are vellus hairs and they help our bodies stay at the right temperature.

Vellus hair

Vellus hairs help us when we are hot.

When we are hot, our sweat coats the vellus hairs. The hairs help the sweat evaporate, letting us cool down.

Smelly Sweat

Sometimes when we sweat, things can get a little bit stinky. But it isn't our sweat that smells. It's the bacteria breaking down our sweat that makes us stink!

It is thought that some foods can make our sweat smell more than others. If you eat a lot of these foods, you might be stinkier than usual.

Sweat Stats

Did you know that hippos have red sweat? It helps protect their skin in the heat by acting like sunscreen.

The sweat also kills harmful bacteria on their skin.

The **average** person will sweat around 48 gallons (183 liters) a year. That's about a whole bath full of sweat!

The maximum amount of sweat a person can produce in a day is 3.7 gallons (14 L)!

Glossary

average: the typical and usual; not outside the ordinary

bacteria: microscopic living things that can cause diseases

glands: a type of organ in the body that produces chemicals

liquid: a material that flows, such as water

minerals: important things that plants, animals, and humans need to grow

odorless: to have no detectable smell

oxygen: a natural gas that most living things need in order to survive

vapor: tiny parts of a solid or liquid that float in the air as a gas, such as mist or steam

viruses: tiny living things that live inside other things and make them ill

Index